The Answers Book for Kids

Book for Kids

Volume 8

22 Questions from Kids on Satan & Angels

KEN HAM &
BODIE HODGE

Third Printing: December 2018

Master Books®
P.O. Box 726
Green Forest, AR 72638

Master Books® is a division of the New Leaf Publishing Group, Inc.

Printed in China

Book design by Terry White

ISBN 13: 978-1-68344-067-3
ISBN 13: 978-1-61458-631-9 (digital)

Library of Congress Control Number: 2017952419

All Scripture references are New King James Version unless otherwise noted.

Please visit our website for other great titles: www.masterbooks.com

When you see this icon, there will be related Scripture references noted for parents to use in answering their children's, and even their own, questions.

For Parents and Teachers

Dear parents:

As we dive into this final book of the series, let's reflect on the previous books' questions. There were multitudes of them! Kids have a lot of questions and this is a good thing. So we really need to be diligent in giving them biblical answers.

Regardless of the questions children may ask, we want to encourage you to open the Bible and search for the correct answer. This is what we love to do. And our hope is that you will have that same love for truth of the Bible. God's Word is always true and this is something in which we can rest assured.

When it comes to Satan and angels, God is our only reliable source of information. Are you ready to see the questions we received from the kids? Here we go!

Blessings in Christ,

Ken and Bodie

Question: Is there one angel or many, and do we know any of their names?

Tyler and Isabella

Ages 10 & 7

4

Answer:

Or do you think that I [Jesus] cannot now pray to My Father, and He will provide Me with more than twelve legions of angels? (Matthew 26:53).

God is our only reliable source of information about angels. In the Bible, angel means "messenger," and they are spirits (Hebrews 1:14). This means they do not have bodies like we do.

There are many angels, and Jesus tells us about legions of them. A legion was usually no less than about 6,000 soldiers. Jesus gave us a clue that at least 72,000 angels were at His command for this one instance if He wanted them. The point is that there are a lot of angels. There were different types of messengers (angels) in the Bible. In some cases, even the Lord was the messenger, being the *Angel of the Lord* (Genesis 16:7–13).

The Bible reveals only two names of angels. One of them was Michael — a chief angel, which is also called an "archangel." He was chief over a group of other angels (Jude 1:9; Revelation 12:7).

Another angel was Gabriel. He helped Daniel understand his vision in the Old Testament. He was also the angel who brought good news to Mary that she was to be the mother of baby Jesus. Sometimes, people have suggested names for other angels, but these names do not come from the Bible.

Luke 1:19; Jude 1:9;
Revelation 12:7

HOLY BIBLE

Question: Do angels have halos and wings?

Becca and Ethan

Answer:

One wing of the cherub was five cubits, and the other wing of the cherub five cubits: ten cubits from the tip of one wing to the tip of the other (1 Kings 6:24).

The Bible doesn't mention halos. There is much history about the halo both from Christian and non-Christian sources. When dealing with halo art, Christians usually view it as symbolizing the "light of the world" and "crown of glory" that shines from Christ, Christians, and angels. Again, this has to do with art, not necessarily reality.

Angelic beings, like the ones in our verse, can also be called a cherub or cherubim (plural). Even though angels are spiritual beings, God describes the cherubim as having wings and hands.

A nice description of cherubim is given in the Bible. They were to be figurines on the "Ark of the Covenant," also called the "Ark of the Testimony," which held the Ten Commandments (it was a fancy box!). Their wings extended over the "mercy seat," which was like a lid that sat on top of the Ark of the Covenant.

God also placed cherubim at the entrance to the Garden of Eden to keep man from returning to the Tree of Life in Genesis 3. This was after Adam and Eve sinned and were kicked out of the Garden. These cherubim were armed with flaming swords!

Exodus 25:20; Ezekiel 10:8

7

Question:

What do angels do besides singing?

Tyler & Becca

Ages 10 & 9

8

Answer:

Praise Him, all His angels; praise Him, all His hosts! (Psalm 148:2).

Angels are ministering spirits (Hebrews 1:14). Therefore, they minister (preach)! After Jesus was temped by Satan, angels came and ministered to Jesus (Matthew 4:11).

Angels also do other things, like giving messages. This was the case with Gabriel giving Mary the message that she would be the mother of Jesus (Luke 1:26–38). An angel gave messages to Elijah too (2 Kings 1:3).

Another thing angels did was to enact judgment and fight in war (e.g., 2 Chronicles 32:21; Revelation 12:7). Angels also praise God (Psalm 148:2). When Jesus was born, hosts of heavenly beings (which included angels) praised God (Luke 2:13). These are just a few of the tasks that God created angels to perform.

Interestingly, there is something that angels do not do. Angels do not get married! Jesus mentioned this in Matthew 22:30. Also, we are not to pray to angels since Jesus is our only mediator ("go between") to God (1 Timothy 2:5). We are not to worship angels either since God alone is to be worshiped (Revelation 19:10, 22:8–9).

Hebrews 1:13–14; 2 Samuel 24:16;
1 Kings 1:15

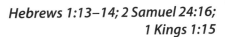

9

Question:

If Satan was an angel and turned bad, does that mean there are other bad angels?

Jaden

Age unknown

10

Answer:

So the great dragon was cast out, that serpent of old, called the Devil and Satan, who deceives the whole world; he was cast to the earth, and his angels were cast out with him (Revelation 12:9).

The Bible describes Satan (who is also called the devil, great dragon, or Lucifer) as being among the heavenly host. He was also called a cherub (Ezekiel 28:14), so this means he could be called a type of angel.

When Satan fell, it was due to his pride to ascend above God to be God. Originally, Satan was created perfect, like all of creation (Genesis 1:31; Deuteronomy 32:4), but when sin was found in him, he was cast out.

The Bible says in Revelation 12:7: "And war broke out in heaven: Michael [*an archangel*] and his angels fought with the dragon [Satan]; and the dragon and his angels fought."

When Satan rebelled and his angels with him, they were all cast out of heaven. Sometimes, angels were "*metaphorically*" equated with stars or "*luminaries*" (things that shine in the sky). In Revelation 12:3–4, Satan (the great dragon) caused one-third of the stars (angels) to fall from heaven. The bad angels are often equated with demons now.

When it comes down to it, Satan and his angels (who are all created beings) have no power next to the all-powerful Creator God.

2 Peter 2:4; Jude 1:6

11

Question: Why did God create the devil when He knew that he would turn against Him and against people too?

Reese and Sarah

Ages 9 & 7

12

Answer:

He who sins is of the devil, for the devil has sinned from the beginning. For this purpose the Son of God was manifested, that He might destroy the works of the devil (1 John 3:8).

God always had a plan, and God always knew what would happen. God knows all things, so Satan's rebellion was not a "surprise" to God (Psalm 147:5).

God's plan works in spite of Satan's sin and rebellion. God can use all things to work for the good of those who love Him (Romans 8:28). When Satan sinned, and then used a serpent to deceive Eve (and then Adam) into sin (Genesis 3), God already had a plan in place to rescue sinners through His Son Jesus (Genesis 3:15).

The Bible says that Jesus (the Lamb) was slain from the beginning (Revelation 13:8). This means that God always knew Satan would sin and lead man into rebellion. Christ had a plan to lay down His life for those who love God, and take His life back up again (John 10:17–18).

Satan only has a little time to deceive man, and then his time is up. He will be cast into the "lake of fire" or "hell" forever, which was prepared for him (Matthew 25:41). Then those who love Christ, who is God, will live eternally without sin, death, or Satan to destroy things.

Matthew 25:41; Romans 8:28

Question: Why did Satan lie to Eve?

Zachary

Age 6

14

Answer:

We know that we are of God, and the whole world lies under the sway of the wicked one (1 John 5:19).

When Satan sinned, he decided to go after God's most prized creation — mankind. Satan was created during creation week (like all other created things — Colossians 1:16). He witnessed God creating man in God's own image. He saw God give man dominion (to rule) over earth.

Satan tried to overthrow God in heaven because he wanted to rule. Satan sinned and was cast out of heaven (to earth). When Satan sinned, it only affected him as well as those angels that sinned with him.

Then Satan used a serpent for the purpose of deceiving Eve (and ultimately Adam). It wasn't by accident. Satan intentionally attacked those who ruled over the earth. Just like he tried to rule in heaven, he tried to rule on earth by tempting Eve to follow his deception instead of following God. John 8:44 says that Satan is the "father of lies."

Sadly, Eve and Adam both stumbled and disobeyed God, just like Satan wanted. So man sinned. This is why the world "lies under the sway of the wicked one." Satan attacked God — and Adam and Eve whom God loved. Today, we still see Satan attacking people that God loves.

John 8:44; 1 John 3:8

Question: Why does Satan hate God?

Zachary

Age 6

Answer:

But he who sins against me wrongs his own soul; all those who hate me love death (Proverbs 8:36).

God is the life (John 14:6). Satan sinned against God. This proved that he loved death more than he loved life. As Satan's love for death grew more and more, his new hate for God grew more and more. Satan is consumed with hate like a fire (Ezekiel 28:18).

Satan's hatred for God extends to man because we are made in God's image. And God loves us. So Satan is the personal adversary of both God and man. The Bible says to hate evil and love good (Amos 5:15). But Satan loves evil and hates good. All good things come from God so Satan's hatred for God extends to the good things that come from God. When people love Jesus and turn from their sin and wickedness, Satan will not like it. But Jesus said in John 15:18:

If the world hates you, you know that it hated Me before it hated you.

Jesus also said in Luke 6:27:

But I say to you who hear: Love your enemies, do good to those who hate you.

We should mimic God's good love, and not Satan's hate and evil.

John 3:20; James 4:7

Question: Does God love Satan?

Amity

Age unknown

Answer:

He who does not love does not know God, for God is love (1 John 4:8).

Prior to Satan's sin, there would have been no reason to think that God did not love Satan. God is love (1 John 4:8). And God's "very good" creation in six days included Satan (Genesis 1:31; Exodus 20:11). So it makes sense that God indeed loved Satan.

When Satan chose disobedience (sin) against God, Satan became the father of lies, sin, and evil. Does God love these things? Not at all. God hates lying, sin, and evil (Proverbs 6:16–19), and we should be the same way (Psalm 97:10).

We should hate evil and sin. Hate can be a good or bad thing depending on what we are talking about. You should not hate your family or God or good and righteous things, but you should hate evil and sin.

Have there been examples in your life where you loved sin more than God? If so, you should repent (be sorry and turn from that sin). Satan did not repent, and he never will. God knows the future and told us that Satan will be punished forever because of his sin (Revelation 20:10). This means Satan will never repent.

Proverbs 6:16–19; Psalm 97:10

19

Question:

Animals can't talk, so how could the serpent talk?

Meagan and Talia

Ages 9 & 7

Answer:

Now the serpent was more cunning than any beast of the field which the LORD God had made. And he said to the woman, "Has God indeed said, 'You shall not eat of every tree of the garden'?" (Genesis 3:1).

Actually, some animals, like many birds, do "talk"! But they don't make sense. For example, a blue-fronted Amazon parrot has the ability to speak. It mimics things that were already said, but a bird mimicking speech doesn't understand the meaning behind what is said.

When the serpent that was in the Garden of Eden was originally created, it obviously had an ability to speak (not sure about other serpents). Being an animal, though, it was limited in its intelligence. It could be clever, cunning, or crafty, but not like a human who is made in God's image.

When Satan influenced the serpent to speak, then it made sense to Eve (the words had meaning). It wasn't because the serpent understood language, but it was Satan speaking lies through the serpent, who was used as a "vessel."

The original serpent was cursed to crawl on its belly and eat dust as part of its new diet (Genesis 3:14). The serpent's original body was changed due to the Curse. Its ability to talk was lost. Whether all serpents originally had the ability to speak, we don't know. We know that living serpents today can't "talk."

Genesis 3:14; 2 Corinthians 11:3

21

Question: Do angels ever come down to earth?

Paige

Age 10

22

Answer:

So Jacob went on his way, and the angels of God met him (Genesis 32:1).

Besides Jacob, there are several examples in the Bible where God permitted angels to be seen and do things on earth. There were two angels that came with the Lord to rescue Lot when God destroyed some evil cities called Sodom and Gomorrah. This was in the Book of Genesis, chapter 19.

In Numbers 22:31–35, we read about an angel who confronted a man named Baalam. Even King David saw an angel (2 Samuel 24:17).

Gabriel was probably the most famous angel encounter. Gabriel was the angel who gave Mary the message that she was favored of God to bring Jesus the Messiah into the world (Luke 1:26–33).

The Bible says that some people are visited by angels and they don't even realize it! The Book of Hebrews says:

Do not forget to entertain strangers, for by so doing some have unwittingly entertained angels (Hebrews 13:2).

When angels appear to people, they look like people, but this doesn't mean they are human. People (mankind) are descendants of Adam and angels are not — they are still angels and will return to their original spiritual form.

Luke 1:26–33

HOLY BIBLE

Question: What happened to Satan at the beginning?

Walton

Age 10

Answer:

*You were perfect in your ways from the day you were created, till iniquity was found in you (Ezekiel 28:15).

Satan was originally perfect and without sin. God created things perfectly (Deuteronomy 32:4) and His creation was very good (Genesis 1:31), including Satan. He was without sin, until the day that he did sin (Ezekiel 28:15).

Satan sinned of his own desire. James 1:14–15 says:

But each one is tempted when he is drawn away by his own desires and enticed. Then, when desire has conceived, it gives birth to sin; and sin, when it is full-grown, brings forth death.

Satan was drawn away by his own desire and his own pride to ascend above the throne of God (Isaiah 14:12–14). He wanted to be God. Because of this, he sinned and has been judged.

This is why Satan has been cast out of heaven and is reserved for hell for all eternity. Hell is separation from God and, moreover, His goodness. We know the beginning of Satan, and we know what will happen to him in the future — everlasting death apart from God's blessings.

*This is directed to Satan who was influencing the King of Tyre in Ezekiel.

Ezekiel 28:15; Isaiah 14:12-14

Question: Why did Satan choose to use a serpent?

Audrey

Age 10

Answer:

But I am afraid that just as Eve was deceived by the serpent's cunning, your minds may somehow be led astray from your sincere and pure devotion to Christ (2 Corinthians 11:3 ESV).

Satan's act of using a serpent may have been for several reasons. The Bible says the serpent was cunning — which means clever or smart.

When God made animals, they varied in their intelligence. In other words, some animals were clever, and some were not as clever. But all of them were created with the level of intelligence to perfectly do what they were created to do. For example, a platypus was created with the ability to swim and the intellect to do it properly. A chicken was not gifted with swimming, nor the intellect to do so!

The serpent was *more cunning* than other beasts of the field. So this may be one reason Satan used the serpent.

Another reason could be that the serpent originally had the ability to speak "phonically" or out loud. This was so that Satan could use the serpent to speak to Eve to try to deceive her.

Another possibility is that the serpent may have been the only animal near Eve when Satan decided to try to deceive her. There could be other reasons too.

Genesis 3:1;
Revelation 12:9, 20:2

Question: Can angels become demons?

Raymond

Age 11

28

Answer:

Now the Spirit expressly says that in latter times some will depart from the faith, giving heed to deceiving spirits and doctrines of demons (1 Timothy 4:1).

The Bible doesn't directly tell us that fallen angels became demons, but this is what most people believe. There are good reasons for this. When Satan fell, one-third of the angels joined his rebellion and fell. These spiritual beings now have a fallen and sinful nature.

Demons follow Satan (Matthew 12:25–28 — Beelzebub in this passage is one of Satan's names). Demons have an "unclean" or fallen nature and are spirits (e.g., Luke 4:33; 1 Timothy 4:1). Like the fallen angels, they will be tormented in hell when the time comes (Matthew 8:28, 25:41). As you can see, there is a good reason to view demons as fallen angels.

In the same way that Satan can have several names like the Devil, Lucifer, and Beelzebub, so fallen angels can also go by other names like demons, unclean spirits, and deceiving spirits. These names are often "interchangeable" with each other.

We don't have a problem calling fallen angels demons, deceiving spirits, and so on. The Bible talks about angels that did not rebel with Satan and chose to remain with God. We will discuss them in the next question.

Luke 11:18–20

HOLY BIBLE

Question:

If angels were perfect and in heaven, how could they sin?

Reena & Paige

Ages 10 & 9

Answer:

The devil, who deceived them, was cast into the lake of fire and brimstone where the beast and the false prophet are… (Revelation 20:10).

Like man, angels were given freedom to think and make decisions for themselves. Man had the option to obey God and refuse to eat from the Tree of the Knowledge of Good and Evil. Adam and Eve disobeyed God. They sinned, and we have to deal with the consequences of sin ever since it happened in the Garden of Eden about 6,000 years ago (Genesis 3).

Angels had the option to remain with God or follow after Satan when he rebelled against the Lord. Satan rebelled. Angels had the freedom to stand with God or disobey like Satan did.

One-third of the angels (Revelation 12:4) decided to follow Satan and rebel. And they must deal with the consequences. The angels that remained with God are called the "elect angels" (1 Timothy 5:21). These angels *elected* or "decided" to stay with God and oppose Satan and his angels. This means that two-thirds of the angels remained with God.

Fallen angels have no possibility of salvation. They tasted the heavenly gift of being with God and rebelled anyway. Man, being made in the image of God, has been given the means of salvation through Christ's death and Resurrection.

1 Timothy 5:21; Revelation 12:7

31

Question:

If Satan sinned first, why did Adam get the blame?

Reena

Age 10

Answer:

Therefore, just as through one man sin entered the world, and death through sin, and thus death spread to all men, because all sinned (Romans 5:12).

Satan's sin was first but it only affected him. It didn't affect the world. The reason was because Satan was not given dominion over anything that God created.

Man was given "dominion" or "rule" over the earth and the animals in it, according to Genesis 1:26–27. In other words, man was put in charge of the earth, which included all the living creatures on the land, in the sea, and that flew in the air.

Satan turned to man, who did have dominion, to begin his deception with Eve. Then when Adam and Eve sinned, their whole dominion fell with them. This means the whole earth fell with Adam and Eve when they ate from the fruit. When Satan sinned, his sin didn't affect the earth.

But when Adam sinned, it affected everything of which they were put in charge. So the earth was affected and all the animals were affected by sin. Adam gets the blame for this, and the punishment for sin was death. Adam was put in charge of his wife, so he received the ultimate blame for sin in the world in Romans 5:12.

Genesis 1:26–27

Question: Do angels fight with demons?

Annie

Age 10

Answer:

And war broke out in heaven: Michael and his angels fought with the dragon; and the dragon and his angels fought (Revelation 12:7).

We can see from this verse in Revelation that angels indeed fight against rebellious angels. Fallen or evil angels are often equated with demons. Angels are spiritual beings (Hebrews 1:14). Because of this, we are limited in our understanding of these battles.

But we know that God wins. This means the fallen angels or demons do not win. Their ultimate punishment is the lake of fire or hell (Matthew 25:41). This doesn't mean that demons lose every battle (e.g., Acts 19:13–17). Just like battles in war, the enemies can have advances.

In the Bible, we see where demons had possessed people and Jesus had to rebuke them and send them away. It shows the power of Jesus over the beings that He created. Jesus conferred this power to His Apostles to drive out demons.

All of us have been called to resist the devil himself. If we submit to God and resist the devil, whose power has been broken by Jesus, he will flee (James 4:7). Angels and demons fight, but there is one winner — God — with the angels who fight with Him.

Matthew 25:41; James 4:7; Jude 1:9

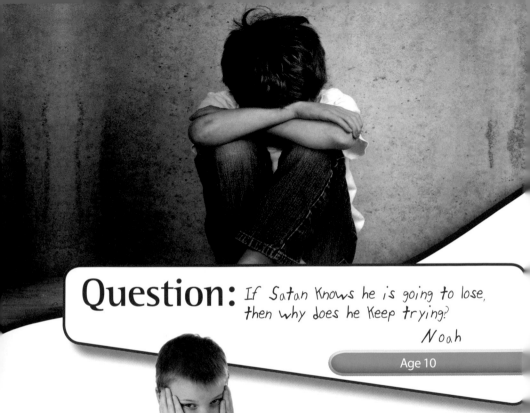

Question: If Satan knows he is going to lose, then why does he keep trying?

Noah

Age 10

Answer:

To the pure all things are pure, but to those who are defiled and unbelieving nothing is pure; but even their mind and conscience are defiled (Titus 1:15).

Satan is consumed with evil. As a result, he is no longer in his "right mind" because his own sin has corrupted or warped his mind. He knew what heaven was like with all of its goodness, but he rejected it because of his own pride. Now Satan's desire is to lash out at God and bring as many people down to hell as he can.

But they traded heaven for sin by betraying God. God knew they would sin. It didn't take God by surprise. Satan, fallen angels, and demons cannot change that sinful nature that they now have (i.e., *mind and conscience is defiled or "messed up"*).

With man's fallen nature, we can be changed and redeemed by Jesus Christ. We can once again be sanctified (made "holy" or "pure" by the Holy Spirit) because Christ's righteousness becomes our righteousness. It is transferred to us (Romans 4:22–24).

Because Satan has a fallen nature that will not be redeemed, his mind is warped and distorted and cannot realize that whatever he does, it will not thwart God. So his own fallen nature prevents him from being able to stop. Satan will no longer be an adversary to God and man when he is finally cast into hell (Revelation 20:10).

James 1:13–15

HOLY BIBLE

Question: What do the devil and demons look like?

Grant

Age 7

Answer:

You were the anointed cherub who covers; I established you; you were on the holy mountain of God; you walked back and forth in the midst of fiery stones (Ezekiel 28:14).

Very little is given in the Bible about the appearance of demons. This makes sense. Satan and demons are spiritual, so we don't really know what they would look like in the physical world.

We are given a brief description by God of cherubim, which are a spiritual type of "angels." This is how they would look if they were physical. They had a face and wings, for example. Satan was called an "anointed cherub" in Ezekiel 28:14. Thus, it is possible that the cherub description would also fit Satan, unless his spiritual appearance had changed due to sin and the Curse in Genesis 3.

When spiritual beings are described in human or physical terms, it is called "personification." This is often done to relate the nature of spiritual beings to man — like God having hands, a back, and a face (Exodus 33:20–23). The Bible tells us a lot about the actions of demons and the devil, but the Bible is silent on what these spiritual beings look like.

Exodus 33:20–23

Question:
Did the serpent have legs?

Grace

Age 11

Answer:

So the LORD God said to the serpent: "Because you have done this, you are cursed more than all cattle, and more than every beast of the field; on your belly you shall go, and you shall eat dust all the days of your life (Genesis 3:14).

Animals, including the serpent, were cursed by God as a result of sin. In Genesis 3, we know that the serpent would crawl on its belly. The Bible doesn't say if the serpent originally had legs or not. Today, most serpents whether snakes, lizards, legless lizards, komodo dragons, or crocodiles, crawl on their belly.

Some of these animals have legs and some do not. Yet, all crawl on their bellies. Some think that the serpent had legs but was changed to have no legs. Some think its legs were merely shortened or changed. A few others think the serpent didn't have legs before or after the Curse. If the serpent was already crawling on its belly before the Curse, then what would the point of the Curse be?

So likely, it had legs originally, because there were other physical changes going on at the Curse as well. For example, some plants changed to have thorns and thistles and Eve (and all women after her) would have pain when having children. There were many physical changes occurring as a result of sin and the Curse.

Isaiah 65:25; Micah 7:17

41

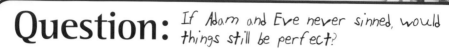

Question: If Adam and Eve never sinned, would things still be perfect?

Jackson

Age 9

42

Answer:

Therefore, just as through one man sin entered the world, and death through sin, and thus death spread to all men, because all sinned (Romans 5:12).

That is a great question! If Adam and Eve's descendants hadn't eaten either, then yes, things would still be perfect. But someone was bound to sin and eat the fruit of the Tree of the Knowledge of Good and Evil.

Keep in mind that God, who made man in His image, allowed man to freely choose (Genesis 2:16). Adam and Eve chose to eat and sinned against God (Genesis 3:6).

God knows all things (Psalm 147:5; Colossians 2:3). God already had a plan in place to save us even before Adam sinned. The Bible says Jesus was "slain from the foundation of the world" (Revelation 13:8). In other words, Jesus knew He would die on the Cross before Adam even sinned.

God always knew that man would sin and we would be in need of a Savior to save us from sin and death. Jesus died the death that we deserve for our sin. Jesus, being God, was able to satisfy God's wrath on sin. This is what makes salvation possible. No one else is capable of taking on the world's sin for *all* time except Jesus. Have you received Jesus Christ as Savior?

Genesis 2:16; Revelation 13:8

SATAN

Question: What was Satan's original name?

Tallia

Age 9

Answer:

Then Jesus said to him, "Away with you, Satan! For it is written, 'You shall worship the LORD your God, and Him only you shall serve'" (Matthew 4:10).

Satan goes by many names. So do we! We can go by our first name, middle name, or last name (Mr. Hodge or Mr. Ham, for example). Or we can go by nicknames or shortened names like Ken instead of Kenneth, Dave rather than David, Liz from Elizabeth, or Jon reduced from Jonathan.

Satan goes by other names too. One popular name is "the devil." Other names for Satan include ancient serpent/serpent of old (Revelation 12:9), Abaddon (destruction), Apollyon (destroyer) (Revelation 9:11), Beelzebub/Beelzebul (Matthew 12:27), Belial (2 Corinthians 6:15), and tempter (Matthew 4:3).

Satan is also called the "god of this world/age" (2 Corinthians 4:4), "ruler of this world" (John 12:31), and "father of lies" (John 8:44).

Another name for Satan is Lucifer which means "light bringer" or "Star of the Morning/Morning Star" in Isaiah 14:12. Some believe that Lucifer was a heavenly or angelic name that was taken from Satan when he rebelled. The Bible doesn't say this, so we have to be cautious about it. Even so, Jesus takes the title "Star of the Morning/Morning Star" away from Satan as it is used of Jesus in Revelation 22:16.

Isaiah 14:12; Revelation 22:16

45

Question: When we die, do we become angels?

Gershom

Age 8

Answer:

For if God did not spare the angels who sinned, but cast them down to hell and delivered them into chains of darkness, to be reserved for judgment (2 Peter 2:4).

It is a misconception that when people die, they become angels. Hebrews 12:22–23 points out that in the City of God, the heavenly Jerusalem, it has both angels and people [the "spirits of just men made perfect"]. When Christians, who are also called saints, die and go to heaven, we are finally made "perfect" — this means we no longer sin. In other words, perfected saints are there; but so are the angels of God. We are separate beings, so people do not become angels.

In certain ways, we will be like angels in heaven sharing in God's goodness directly. But we are still distinct. Remember that in the beginning, man was made a little lower than the angels (Psalm 8:5; 2 Peter 2:11). But we are also made in the image of God (Genesis 1:26–27), and for those in Christ who are saved and go to heaven, we are the "bride of Jesus Christ" who is the King of kings. This gives us a very high position. Saints are even put in charge of judging the world and angels (1 Corinthians 6:2–3; 2 Peter 2:4).

Psalm 8:5; 1 Corinthians 6:2–3

Answers Are Always Important!

The Bible is truly filled with some amazing answers for some of our toughest faith questions. The Answers Book for Kids series answers questions from children around the world in this multi-volume series. Each volume will answer over 20 questions in a friendly and readable style appropriate for children 6–12 years old; and each covers a unique topic, including Creation and the Fall; Dinosaurs and the Flood of Noah; God and the Bible; and Sin, Salvation, and the Christian Life, and more!

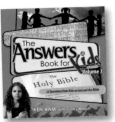

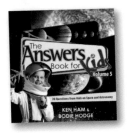

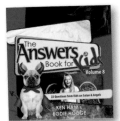